I0166060

Worcester Clark university

Report of the President to the Board of Trustees

Worcester Clark university

Report of the President to the Board of Trustees

ISBN/EAN: 9783743325081

Manufactured in Europe, USA, Canada, Australia, Japa

Cover: Foto ©ninafisch / pixelio.de

Manufactured and distributed by brebook publishing software
(www.brebook.com)

Worcester Clark university

Report of the President to the Board of Trustees

CLARK UNIVERSITY,

WORCESTER, MASS.

First Annual Report of the President

TO THE

BOARD OF TRUSTEES.

Oct. 4, 1890.

WORCESTER, MASS.:
PUBLISHED FOR THE UNIVERSITY.
Nov., 1890.

Gentlemen of the Board of Trustees :—

I have the honor to submit herewith my first annual report.

When called upon to consider the invitation with which the trustees of this university honored me, two and a half years ago, I was in an institution which, in the less than fifteen years of its existence, had done a work in stimulating other institutions, and in advancing the highest standards, which was, as I think all cheerfully admit, beyond comparison in the recent history of higher education in this country. After studying Worcester and the New England situation, I saw the opportunity here to be so great for a further and at least no less epoch-making step, that I felt that assured career, and even an important department, new in this country and full of fascinations, and in the most critical stage of its development, ought not to weigh against it. Permission was at once given me to begin my preparations for this important work by studying foreign institutions for a year. I visited every European country but Portugal, and found everywhere great and surprising advances since my own student life abroad had ended.

The educational awakening in Germany inspired by Fichte after her greatest humiliation by Napoleon was hardly greater than the awakening in France after the catastrophy of 1870. The next year timid partial reforms were proposed in geography and gymnastics, but it was soon seen that the entire system must be recast. Not the schoolmaster who made the soldiers, but the German university which made the schoolmaster, conquered at Sedan, said Renan. If the state is to ensure social order within and be strong without, democracy must find a new principle of life in universities, and education must become the great problem of statesmanship. Before, students had gone direct from the Lycées to technical and special studies. Now studies of a purely scientific character are fostered by stipends, and by the new *École des Hautes Études*, which have for their object to develop savants and professors,—a work formerly left almost solely to the *École Normale.* Formerly instruction was public and to mixed audiences; now seminary and laboratory courses solely for adepts, have excited great enthusiasm and attracted the best and most advanced students all over the country. Formerly the faculties were isolated even in the same town; now, with private, esoteric courses and by the new system of joint councils, and by a policy of concentration, the direct opposite of the English and American method of so called university extension, and by the strange new student fraternities, something like universities, hitherto unknown in France, is the new goal of many lines of endeavor. Twenty new chairs in Paris alone, the greatly enlarged liberties of provincial faculties, and the co-operation of localities in recruiting them, the policy of decentralization in all, but especially in the lower grades of education; the magnificent new *conseil superiéur,* composed of sixty-two leaders in many fields, which brings a wisdom and gives an authority to solutions and measures and is charged with advisory responsibility perhaps the greatest in history; magnificent buildings like the new Sorbonne, the medical school, and Lycées like those of Janson de Sailly and Laon; the establishment of normal schools, five chairs of education in the faculties, of a pedagogical museum, the development of the pedagogy of higher education by several new journals, the docent system; the remarkable new school for the post-graduate training in statesmanship, which, although a private institution, is training the political leaders of all parties; the new law of 1878, basing all clinical and practical medical studies upon the sciences which underlie them (chemistry and the various branches of biology); the Musée Guimet, which two years ago opened its extensive museums and libraries, and now offers facilities for the study of comparative religion unequalled in the world; and the great fact that in fourteen years the total amount devoted to education in that country has increased sevenfold;—all this shows how far, in the words of a distinguished French statesman, higher education is fast becoming the central question for France.

In Italy a council of education, composed of sixteen royal appointees and sixteen professors selected from the universities, has grappled with the problem of subordinating fourteen of its universities to the other seven, which latter are being rebuilt with great and sometimes literally palatial magnificence. As, with the policy of doubling for each provincial university all the funds it can raise for itself, the government has gradually acquired practical control of most of them, scholarly and scientific activity has been awakened to new life in nearly all directions, and ambitions of intellectual leadership, as in the best days of the mediæval universities of Italy, are often manifest.

Holland has revised and co-ordinated her organizations of higher education, and established one new university. Sweden has profoundly reconstructed her educational system on a plan that might be called the most severely modern in the world, and Denmark is taking steps in the same direction. In 1884, Russia after prolonged discussion, re-organized her universities. In Great Britain, new provincial universities, and important changes in the others, too many and great to be briefly described here, have been inaugurated. In Germany, thirteen magnificent university buildings make Strassburg, in all departments, the best of all architectural embodiments of the German university ideal. Halle and Kiel have been, and Breslau is now being, almost entirely rebuilt. New and often magnificent laboratories, libraries, special cliniques, and museums at every seat of learning,—great temples of science, as they were called by one of its perfervid orators, Du Bois-Reymond,—and two single buildings costing four million dollars each, show where much of the French indemnity money has gone ; and what is far more important, the internal has not lagged behind the external growth. At Budapesth, Ghent, Aix-la-Chapelle, Helsingfors in Finland, and even in remote Athens, magnificent new structures show in what esteem science is now held, and what still greater things she is yet expected to do. Several institutions of new pattern, like the Naples School of Zoölogy, which now trains the best professors for Germany; the London University, which is solely an examining body, and does not teach,—these and many more show not only how many and strong, but how differentiated, institutions have become in the field of higher education.

In my trip, information was sought from every source. Books, reports, and building-plans of many kinds were gathered. Ministers of education, heads of universities, and, above all, leading scientific men, were visited. The information and advice of the latter, always cheerfully given, and in not a few cases in detail and in writing, constitute by far the most valuable result of this trip, and will soon be reported on at greater length. Much of this advice was confidential, and involved personalities; some of it embodies long and fondly cherished ideals of great men, nowhere yet realized; but most of it represents the inner aims, methods, and ideals of the best existing institutions, like those named above, and others.

The causes and the effects of all these movements and ideals in Europe have been felt in other lands.

After long discussion, a new university, to which hundreds of Russian patriots with exiled friends have contributed money, household treasures, and even prayers and tears, was at last founded in Siberia, at Tomsk, and not at the chief military centre, where freedom would have been impossible. In Japan one of the most interesting universities in the world has been developed as the centre and instrument of most of the remarkable transformations in that country. In Australia and South America new and vigorous universities have been recently established.

The new movement is already upon us in this country, and many significant facts show that the resultant interest and opportunity here have never been so great. All such facts and tendencies, and many more, opened a clear and broad field for us at Worcester, and unmistakably defined our work as follows :—

1. It must be of the highest and most advanced grade, with special prominence given to original research. This our country chiefly lacks and needs for both its material and educational welfare. This is in the current of all the best tendencies in the best lands, and is the ideal to-day of, I believe, about every scientific man, who is able and in earnest, throughout the world. For this our location offers the rarest opportunities and inducements yet possible in this country.

2. We must not attempt at once to cover the entire field of human knowledge, but must elect a group of related departments of fundamental importance, and concentrate all our care to make these the best possible. Each science has become so vast and manifold that it is impossible to cultivate the frontier of all at a single university. This is more and more recognized abroad, and is still more true under our American system of private endowment than on the European plan, with a national treasury to draw from. If coming universities, instead of imitating, will supplement others, will elect each its group of studies, all the gain in economy and effectiveness which skilled labor has over unskilled will be secured in the field of highest education.

3. For our group we chose at first five fundamental and related sciences. Work in science can be quickest organized. Great libraries and museums, and every thing else that only age can bring, can be dispensed with at first, and a complete outfit of the best apparatus and of all needed books can be gathered in a

short time. Again, this is a practical country, and its industries are sure to depend more and more on the progess of science. So far, we have utilized science with extraordinary ingenuity in our inventions, but have done comparatively little to create or advance it. We desire to make a patriotic endeavor to develop American discoverers as well as inventors. Finally, and above all, science, with its modern methods, has become an unsurpassed school of discipline, culture, and reverence.

4. We must seek the most talented and best trained young men. We must not exploit them for the glory of the institution, work them in a machine, nor retard their advancement, but we must give them every needed opportunity and incentive. Their salaries must be among the very best in the country, yet we must not ask them to spend their best energies in teaching and earning tuition fees for the university, and must leave open all possibilities, should such problems as individual fees, a periodic year in Europe, etc., arise later. We must give to those who know how to value it such facilities as we are able, that they may work for science and for themselves, requiring in return only a limited amount of mutual instruction, special and advanced enough to aid rather than divert from research, (and no one is so eager and so able to teach the few fit as a discoverer), and careful conformity to a few obvious regulations.

As from hundreds of applicants we have admitted but a very few of the best because many would frustrate our plans, so from the many subjects found in most large universities we selected five to receive all our care, although later we hope to increase both.

Mathematics is often called the queen of all the

sciences. As the latter become exact, they approx-
imate it, and are fructified by its spirit and its methods.
Its antiquity, its disciplinary value, its rapid and recent
development, make it obviously indispensable. Physics is the field of the most immediate application of
mathematics, and deals with the fundamental forces of
the world, heat, sound, light, electricity,—and the un-
derlying problems of form and motion generally, with
their vast field of application in such sciences as astron-
omy and dynamic geology. Chemistry, with its great,
sudden development, revealing marvellous order and
harmony in the constitution of matter, is rapidly ex-
tending its dominion over industrial processes. Biology, which seeks to fathom the laws of life, death,
reproduction and disease, that underlies all the medical
sciences, in its broader aspects has taught man in
recent decades far more concerning his origin and
nature than all that was known before. Psychology,
or the study of man's faculties and their education, is
a new field into which all the sciences are now bearing
so many of their richest and best ideas, and now so full
of promise of better things for the life of man. These
five we must have, and nowhere is man brought so
close to the primitive revelation of God in his works.

We have thus sought in these departments the
highest form of what is called the philosophical faculty,
devoted to non-professional specialization. We are not
a 'graduate department' in which most so-called graduate students attend, and most professors conduct
undergraduate work. We are not an institution like
the Smithsonian, which does no teaching. We are not
an academy of sciences, but we have features of all
these, and many more. This work is the most labori-
ous and the most expensive. It is the most all-condi-

tioning and the most central for any and every new departure. An undergraduate department, a medical school, a technical school, and even still more specialization in the existing departments, or new ones of any kind, could be developed from this basis with comparatively little labor, time, and all but the last with little expense. But the value of all professional or industrial schools depends on the vigor and dominance of the philosophical faculty, the heart of every true university, from which they derive their life and light, and where knowledge is pursued for its own sake, and for its culture effect on the investigator.

We are thus a school for professors, where leisure, method, and incentive train select men to higher and more productive efficiency than before.

Last year college trustees elsewhere found a full half-dozen of our fellows only too attractive for their vacant chairs. But if we can thus relieve college trustees of the difficulties under which they sometimes succumb, in selecting suitable men for professorships, we can also ease them of the great expense of providing advanced courses, and from the temptation of retaining after graduation their best men, who could and should utilize larger opportunities.

The rule of receiving only graduates has been steadily adhered to. All but two of our students have had one or more years of study after graduation before entering here. If we are really to relieve colleges of the necessity of attempting university work, we must not place our standards too high, and should receive any earnest man who intends a scientific career immediately after his college course ends. Many graduates, however, are not quite qualified to take up the work of investigation, but, on the other hand, research cannot be successful with large numbers. It requires constant personal intercourse between professor and student at the most critical stage of the latter's development. If he falls into cheap methods and ideals of research, as is too often the case, his career will be vain, useless, and even harmful. Every new research may need new apparatus, expeditions may be necessary, and plans and methods partly carried out may have to be changed, as nature reveals new avenues to her precious secrets.

The relation of the university to the college has the same perplexities as that of the college to the preparatory school. Sometimes young men are not sufficiently trained in college to utilize all the advantages of the university, still less to engage in original research, and sometimes able men are held back in post-graduate courses in small colleges, which do their proper work admirably, but lack the means to offer the far larger and more costly opportunities of the university. The A. B. degree is now a finality for no scholar, and if it be that changes impend that may bring it earlier, and that the incalculable advantages of real university life and work in our own country be opened to more and more of these graduates, then our problem of making a better adaptation of our work to colleges generally and individually becomes increasingly imperative, — the more so, as we are, I believe, the only university in the country which does not draw its chief earnings from and do most of its teaching for undergraduates, and many, if not most of its so-called graduate students, take undergraduate courses. In no university has the proportion of expenditure to income been so high as here, for, although our tuition is higher than any university or college known to me, we can admit but very few students. We must, therefore, give precedence to the very best and make full membership in Clark University an honor. This, however, need not prevent us from abating tuitions in worthy cases, nor even from holding quizzes or brief and special preparatory courses for graduates who are promising but not fully qualified to use to the uttermost the opportunities here, should we later desire to do so.

For those students whom we receive we should do everything possible for instructors to do. They should be personally aided, guided to the best literature, and advanced by every method that pedagogic skill and sympathy can devise. They should feel all the enthusiasm, understand all the interests, and all the methods of the instructor. He should confidentially share with them all his hopes and plans for research. A great leader in science in Europe lately said in substance that he who has reserves from his own select and nearest student-apprentices, and has not learned the wisdom of sharing his choicest ideas freely with those he instructs without fear that they will be appropriated to his detriment, is not himself fertile in ideas, and is a pedagogue rather than a professor. The best and most advanced students will best and keenest and most lastingly appreciate all this, and every other effort in their behalf whether by professors or by the authorities of the university. The chief study of the latter is that every one here be so placed that he may do the best and the most work of which he is capable. They are quick to share the pleasure and pride in his every achievement, and feel every token of appreciation he may receive from the competent expert, or which he in return is sure to feel for their endeavors. Our great work, now in its most interesting, formative stage, when the very highest ideas may not be without some practical results, should inspire all with a passion for harmony and co-operation, and even if need be for forbearance and mutual concession. Perhaps none of us will ever see again an opportunity so precious and for a movement in the field of highest education in this country of great historic and national significance.

Our docents are in no way assistants, and their relations are directly with the president. They are exempt from all routine work, and are independent in both teaching and research. They are expected to work for science and for themselves. These positions have attracted a group of young men of very rare ability and attainment, who are certain to have great influence on the scientific future of this country. To aid them by councils, and to provide for their needs, is not only a rare satisfaction for administrators or professors, but is certain to raise the level of both scientific work and instruction in our country. A new institution naturally attracts young men who, even though not always experienced in the business of faculty meetings and in the details of building and equipment, are the very life of an institution, whose authorities are inspired by their noble ambitions.

In our methods of instruction, stated lectures, which are required by vote of the trustees of each instructor, are the smallest part. Elbow-teaching is given in the laboratory, and there is individual and constant guidance of reading, as well as experimentation, if needed or desired. Clubs, conferences, and seminaries are held, where all important literature in a wide field, and in different languages, is read; each man taking a subject, and reading and reporting for the benefit of others. Not only the information, but the insight, criticism, methods, and standpoint of each are pooled for the edification and stimulation of all. The contact between professor and student was never closer, and more avenues were never opened between minds working in the same place and field.

The most important part of our work is research, and we wish soon to be ready to be chiefly judged by the value of our contributions to the sum of human knowledge. By the unanimous vote of the board of trustees, approved by a unanimous vote of the faculty. the leading consideration in all engagements, re-appointments, and promotions, must be the quality and quantity of successful investigation. This significant step gives us a unique character, and makes most of our problems new ones.

It seems, and often is, a very simple and easy thing to take a free look at new facts. This kind of investigation may be made by any traveller or intelligent collector of specimens. It is sometimes harder to slightly vary the conditions in well-known fields, and note the concomitant variations in the result. Both these kinds of work are, in a sense, original research. Such are many of the theses for the doctor's degree, not to speak of those that are not published; so that the work of the professors and the students, and the standing of the university and the value of its degree, are unknown. Results must be had without risk of failure. Very different from and above this and all so-called 'analogy-work' are the investigations conducted by the aid of accomplished experts, who have already taken their doctor's degree, and give their entire time to co-operation with the professors. Of these we have had one or more in each experimental department during the year, and with excellent results, for investigation. Risks of negative results, often very important in themselves, must be freely taken, if results of great value are to be attained.

There is no institution that should be more respected than a university that is old and large, whether in Europe or America. It has been the home of the best youth in their best years; their highest hopes and choicest memories center in it. It has trained those who made the state great and the church sacred and beneficent. Old men visit it to reanimate old friendships and renew their hold on youth and on ideals. There are great libraries, museums, and buildings and wealth accumulated from many donors. All these things money cannot buy nor new institutions duplicate, if they would. None of us all can love his cherishing mother too warmly, speak too ardently in her praise, or resent too hotly any indignity put upon her.

Yet age which brings wisdom may bring infirmities. In a time and land where change is so rapid Trustees, Alumni and even Faculties sometimes fall behind. Time is lost in administrative details better left to one. Young men are held back, and talent not held to its best thing, but kept doing the work of cheaper men, and the question may become pertinent why, with vast resources, so little is done for culture and for the advancement of knowledge by old institutions or comparatively so much by new ones. There is much to foster complacency, and an unfortunate absence of competent criticism from without whence all university reforms in history have really come.

Prejudices may accumulate from without, and student custom and ideals grow up within that are as inveterate and ineradicable as they are vicious and absurd, but which make progress slow and hard. There is sometimes an excess of conservations, routine, and machinery. Saddest of all, perhaps, departments of endowed knowledge, like professors, sometimes cease to be productive and grow dry, formal, sterile, but they cannot be displaced. It may be harder to regard an old institution as a means, precious only as it broadly serves the highest culture-interests of the whole nation, and not as an end precious in and for itself. We know how wasteful and unproductive the vast resources of Oxford and Cambridge had become in 1854, and what old abuses had to be corrected in Italy and Holland by such and other somewhat drastic outside means. In this new country we need new men, new measures, and occasionally new universities; and we, like England, have in later years experienced their amazing good. In the field of experimental science, unlike some other departments, what is there of importance, that a few centuries can afford, that cannot be at least as well provided in a few years?

We duplicate almost nothing in other universities in this country. A full department of Physics, Chemistry, or Mathematics even, to say nothing of Biology, the complexity of which is more obvious, as sketched for us by several European leaders in their field, would each require several professors, each with one or more assistant professors to represent its several sections or departments of the subject. Thus, to say nothing of difference of grade or standard, it does not follow that because we have Physics, Chemistry, and other depart-

2

ments found in other institutions, there is duplication. The contrary is, in fact, the case. The best professors in these fields, however authoritative they may be in the entire department, excel in and contribute chiefly to but a few chapters of it, leaving ample space for other directions of excellence elsewhere.

In the new era of university development, upon which this country is now entering, it is of fundamental importance for economy and for the success of a great movement, that in place of the monotonous uniformity, duplication and servile immitation that has prevailed, institutions should freely differentiate, and should be known to do so; that above the commendable loyalty to local institutions by their graduates, there should arise the same comparative and critical discrimination of institutions, as of courses in the same institutions under the elective system. Perhaps the chief benefit of the latter has been the stimulus it gave to every professor to make his course so profitable that it should prove attractive to the most of the best students. The same stimulus could be given to institutions by the extension of the elective system to them.

In these and many other ways a new institution in a time and place like the present finds its problems new, and ought to become a new movement.

Our departments and sub-departments are divided into majors and minors. This distinction is not based upon the merit or ability of the instructors; some of our best men representing at present minor departments in which we should hesitate to attempt to qualify for the doctor's degree. Neither does it rest upon the scientific importance of the subjects, some of the minors being quite as necessary for a complete university as some of the major departments. It is due essentially to the fact that we are organizing slowly. Enlargements, when they come, which, by vote of the trustees are to be made in departments most closely related to those already established, may any time convert minors into major departments.

The more advanced men here fall into two categories, the staff and the annual appointees. This line of demarcation may not always distinguish greater age, attainment, ability or salary, or general desirability for our work from less. Some annual appointees are older, have done more work and may receive more pay than the lowest on the staff. Each member of the latter has a longer term of appointment, and participates in the hitherto very slight business of faculty administration. The distinction does not coincide with the line between major and minor departments, nor is it due to any doubt about the permanent desirability of the majority of the men now holding these appointments, but it rests now upon certain exigencies of our situation. While it is without doubt a source of stimulation, and to some extent will remain indispensable so long as we are engaged in selecting our faculty, the fact that so many men of great merit are dependent on an annual renewal of their appointment is a source of grave disadvantage, which I venture to express the hope may soon be obviated.

It is impossible, in untechnical terms, to even speak of the researches undertaken here during the year, although these are the chief work of the university. New minerals in Arkansas, with a book on the petrography of that State; chemical action as affected by electricity in the field of a strong magnet; the crystal structure of isomorphous compounds; the ultimate atomic and molecular constitution of two widely different groups of chemical substances, which is said to establish new and important scientific conclusions; further developments of the non-euclidean geometry; several papers, said to be of much algebraic importance, on matrices; a standard of length in terms of a light-wave one fifty-thousandth of an inch long; a new method of greatly magnifying the power of telescopes, so that possibly the disks of fixed stars may be seen (a method speedily put in operation by the Lick Observatory, with the largest telescope glass in the world); the electrical properties of the air, and a little group of problems in meteorology; the embryology of an animal peculiar to America, and of great importance to the ancestry of vertebrate life; studies of sea-anemone and jelly-fishes; the breeding-habits and embryology of the lobster, strangely unknown before; a third fundamental tissue determined for most organs in the vertebrate body; the discovery of the innervation of veins; the comparative study of organs of taste in many vertebrates; fatigue, studied experimentally and also histologically, in the living cell; the brain of the world-known deaf-mute, Laura Bridgman, more thoroughly studied than any brain ever before has been; the time of the quickest mental and nerve processes; the sense of rhythm, so fundamental to several arts; the myths, customs, and beliefs of the native Indian tribes of British Columbia,—all of these and half a dozen more of less significance, some not yet completed, some already published in several languages, represent some of our work here during the past year, so important that if, instead of marking the beginning of a second year with greater facilities and increased numbers and zeal, this occasion marked the close of the university, the sum of human knowledge would have been larger for our having existed, and we should have our place forever in the history of the advancement of science.

In addition to this, I do not here mention the marked stimulus we have already exerted on other institutions on which much might be said, nor the unsought and unexpected public commendation of our plan by a number of the leaders of educational thought in Europe.

During the past year we have received from a " citizen of Worcester " a fund of five thousand dollars to aid " some one or more worthy native born citizens, of the city of Worcester, who may desire to avail himself of the advantages of the institution. Mrs. Eliza W. Field has given five hundred dollars to provide for the minor needs of a scholar or fellow.

Our present needs are the strengthening of some of our existing departments, several new departments and buildings, the enlargement of our library, the equipment of a large room for a gymnasium, especially for winter use, additional fellowships and scholarships.

The work of the university began a year ago, in all its departments. During the first part of the year, the work of furnishing and equipment was carried on side by side with lectures and scientific work. Some unavoidable delay was caused by the tardy filling of orders for books and particularly apparatus. Our nearly threescore men (selected in part only from about nine hundred applicants for various positions) included graduates of forty-eight different universities and colleges. The printed register describes the buildings, grounds, and organization of the faculty; the system of docents and fellowships; methods and courses of instruction; and the scientific and literary equipment of each department. The plans of the founder and some of the conceptions of the trustees and president are printed in a pamphlet containing a report of the opening exercises of the university Oct. 2, 1889. During the year twenty-eight professors and other instructors have given thirty-three courses, attended often by other professors. This method of mutual instruction has proven a great and wholesome stimulus.

In a new movement of such magnitude and importance, we must go slowly to go surely. For many of our new problems there is little precedent in this country to aid us, and in studying the experience of older and more advanced countries, we cannot distinguish too carefully between elements which owe their success to the national spirit, and the different environment of race, religion, industry, tradition, etc., which it would be affectation and folly to attempt to imitate, and those elements which are simply means to an end, which only long experience can evolve, and which it would be as unwise not to avail ourselves of, as to refuse to utilize a mechanical invention because it was of foreign origin.

To do this requires time and much discriminating labor. To bring to bear upon our problems the light and fructifying suggestions of all available experience and wisdom, and thus to aid ourselves in this work, as well as for our students, we begin this year to develop the pedagogy of higher education by a new third journal now about to be issued from the university. For this much preparation has been made in collecting recent literature, reports, laws, etc., and getting access to the best sources of information, both personal and official in Europe and this country, and the results will be digested in each number with as great completeness and conciseness as possible. The journal will be intended also as a convenient aid to the few leaders elsewhere charged with administrative responsibilities in the field of higher education.

While, however, we must go slowly we cannot afford to go too slowly. The present opportunity is without precedent in our educational history. Never were educational opinions so plastic and formative, or all minds so receptive, or so bent on better things in higher education as now. On several important next steps the information is all in and digested, and we are all agreed, and serious loss and grave disappointment of great expectation, which many years will be required to efface will, I am fully convinced, follow long delay. The present opportunity to set noble fashions, to give the right direction to strong and important currents without, possibly no less valuable than the be stand most we dare hope or wish for ourselves within, is precious and cannot last.

Finally, although we yet lack all the traditions and enthusiasm that come with age, with what gratitude and earnest felicitation does every mind and heart here turn to a founder who is not a tradition, a picture, a statue, or even a memory, but the living, animating power of the institution he has planted with such wisdom, and watered with such care! As an investigator toils to bless mankind with new discoveries, so he has wrought that the world might be blessed by the more rapid increase and diffusion of truth. As a teacher longs to impart all his knowledge to a favored pupil, so he has been the best of all my teachers in things in which a scholar may sometimes lack wisdom. As parents are anxious for the comfort and highest success of all their children, so he, and his devoted wife, could even be careless of what all others may say or do, if only every man here be so placed, furnished, and incited as to do the best work of which he is capable, for himself and for science. If we labor with his persistence and devotion, his care in things that are small as well as great, we cannot fail to realize his and all our highest hopes and best wishes for Clark University.

The following reports from the departments cover only the original researches undertaken here during the past year. The teaching, equipment and buildings are described in the Register.

G. STANLEY HALL,

President of the University.

Worcester, Mass., Oct. 4, 1890.

I.—MATHEMATICS.

PROFESSOR STORY.

It will perhaps make clearer what my research-work during the past year has been if I sketch briefly the history of the subject in which I have been working.

No real improvement in geometrical methods was made from the time of Euclid to that of Legendre. In attempting to put the treatment of geometry on a surer logical basis, Legendre, assuming that the straight line is of infinite length, proved that the sum of the angles of a plane triangle cannot exceed two right angles, but he did not succeed in showing that this sum may not fall short of two right angles. Gauss then showed that a consistent geometry could be built upon the assumption that the above-mentioned sum is less than two right angles, and such a geometry he called "non-euclidean." Lobatchefsky and J. Bolyai also independently discovered this geometry, which the former called "imaginary" (now commonly called "hyperbolic geometry"). In 1859, Professor Cayley ("Sixth Memoir upon Quantics," Phil. Trans., Vol. 149) showed that, in the geometry of Euclid, the distance between two points admits of a projective expression and suggests a generalization. Laguerre, in 1853, (Nouvelles annales de Math.) had already given a similar expression for the angle between two lines. From the investigations of Riemann ("Ueber die Hypothesen, welche der Geometrie zu Grunde liegen," Habilitationsschrift read 1854, printed in the Göttinger Abhandlungen, Vol. 13) and Helmholtz ("Ueber die Thatsachen, welche der Geometrie zu Grunde liegen," Göttinger Nachrichten, 1868, No. 6) follows that a consistent geometry can be built on the assumption that the straight line is of finite length, in which geometry the sum of the angles of a plane triangle is greater than two right angles ("elliptic geometry"). In 1871, Professor Klein ("Ueber die sogenaunte Nicht-Euklidische Geometrie," Math. Annalen, Vol. 4) gave

expressions for the most general measures of distances between points and angles between lines and planes which inter-
sect, which are simple generalizations of the expressions
given by Laguerre and Cayley. Beltrami had shown ("Sag-
gio di interpretazione della Geometria non-euclidea," Giorn.
di Matematiche, 1868) that the non-euclidean (hyperbolic)
geometry in a plane is equivalent to the euclidean geometry
on a surface of negative curvative, and, in 1872, Professor
Klein (Math. Ann., Vol. 6) showed the equivalence of the
elliptic and hyperbolic geometries with his projective measurement. In a series of articles published several years ago
in the American Journal of Mathematics, I applied Professor
Klein's definitions to plane and spherical trigonometry (Professor Cayley had already applied them to a *special* plane
trigonometry), extended them to the measurement of areas
and volumes, and gave a number of special applications, particularly to conic sections.

For some time I have had in mind to develop the subject
systematically, applying it to the metrical relations of plane
curves and surfaces in general. During the past year this has
been my principal work. I had hoped to have a memoir
embodying my results ready for publication before this, but
the elaboration of certain parts of the theory, whose very existence was unforeseen, has delayed the work, at the same time
increasing its interest. For the sake of completeness I have
reproduced Professor's Klein's deduction of generalized measurement and the really fundamental formulæ of my former
papers. I have treated the theory of parallels and parallelo-
grams with sufficient thoroughness to show how the
corresponding portion of Euclid is affected. This treatment
suggested (or necessitated) the study of a surface (mentioned
by Clifford) which is defined as the locus of a straight line
moving parallel to itself so as always to meet a given straight
line, and which turns out to be a (non-euclidean) circular
cylinder and (as is sufficiently curious) the only non-
euclidean cylinder of the second order. I was thus led to
study systems of concentric circular cylinders and cylinders
of higher orders, of which I have obtained a number of interesting properties. I have also developed a non-euclidean

theory of the curvature of surfaces. The projective character of the generalized measurement makes a purely geometrical treatment of the subject possible, a fact of which I have made some use, although in general I have employed the analytical method. The analytical theory is however essentially independent of any geometrical application and, regarding results not common to all possible geometrical interpretations as unessential, I have considered as far as I could the true (essential) significance of the infinite and imaginary in geometry, conceptions derivable in the first instance, as it seems to me, only from analysis.

In addition to this work on non-euclidean geometry, I have done something during the latter part of the year toward generalizing the theory of restricted algebraic equations, but the work is not yet in such a shape as to make a statement of results possible.

DR. BOLZA.

The object of my paper published in the American Journal of Mathematics, Vol. 13, is to give a new exposition of the theory of substitutions and its applications to algebraic equations and to supplement the existing treatises on the subject (Jordan, Serret, Netto) in several points.

(1). I try to give an elementary introduction into the somewhat abstract theory of substitutions by presenting it in continual connection with the problem of solution of algebraic equations by radicals, beginning with the solution of the cubic and biquadratic equations.

(2). I lay special stress on the consideration of a substitution group as a special case of groups of operations in general.

HENRY TABER.

During the academic year, 1889–1890, I published a paper in the *American Journal Mathematics*, vol. 12, on the Theory of Matrices. In this paper, I regard a matrix as an operator linear in and distributive over the units of an algebra, and consequently as substantially identical with Hamilton's linear vector operator. By means of this conception, I obtain a very simple development of the subject, including

Cayley's identical equation and Sylvester's most important theorems (law of nullity, law of latency, the corollary of the laws of nullity, and the formula for any function of a matrix.) The object of this paper was to develop the subject, as left by Sylvester, from this very simple point of view: in addition I have completed the investigation of the corollary of the law of nullity for any relation between the latent roots; I have thoroughly treated the matrical roots of unity, and the matrical roots of zero; and I have shown that there is an infinity of algebras constituting a sequel to quaternions and nonions, whose laws of combination are equivalent to those of matrices of prime order. I have also shown that the laws of combination of matrices of composite order are identical with those of algebras whose units are the products of the units of linear algebras analogous to quaternions and nonions: whence it follows that the theory of all linear associative algebras is included in that of sets of quaternions, such that the units of one set are commutative with those of another. In addition I have extended the conception of the quaternion symbols S and V to the theory of matrices in general. And in regard to the effect of the linear vector operator upon its ground, I have shown that what I term the latent regions of the matrix constitute subordinate grounds: i. e., that the effect of the matrix upon any vector in the extension pertaining to any latent root is to translate the quantity into one in the same extension; and that this property is true of any rational integral function of the matrix.

During the academic year, 1889–1890, I continued the investigations of this paper, and the results are embodied in one paper, shortly to appear in print, and in two others nearly ready for publication. The first paper entitled *"On Certain Identities in the Theory of Matrices,"* will appear in the next number of the *American Journal of Mathematics.* In this paper I have given a new proof (without employing the conception of a linear vector operator) of the extension to matrices in general of the quaternion symbols S and V. I have applied this extension to the chain of equations, and shown how, without employing Sylvester's latent function of the corpus of two matrices, from either of the identical equations of two matrices, to obtain by immediate differentiation the other identical relations of their catena ; and I have shown that the coefficients of the catena may be expressed in terms of the sums of the latent roots of the products of powers of the matrices involved, and given the expression for the coefficients of the catena in the case of matrices of the second and third orders. In addition I have shown how the identical equation, Sylvester's interpolation theorem, and the law of latency may be made to appear as explicit identities by employing the conception of the conjugate extended to matrices in general.

Since the close of the academic year, 1889–1890, I have completed a paper on the application to the theory of matrices of the symbols S and V. It is now ready for publication. It contains a simpler proof of the extension to matrices of any order of the symbols S and V, and a simpler method of applying these symbols to the catena of any number of matrices; in addition it contains the solution of a problem in matrices proposed by Sylvester*, and an expression for the involutant of two matrices in terms of the sums of the latent roots of the products of powers of the two matrices, also a simple demonstration that the latent roots of two matrices are the same in whatever order they may be joined multiplicatively.

---

*The problem is, given two nonions, i and j, such that $i^3 = j^3 = 1$ and $ji = \lambda i j$ (where λ is an imaginary cube root of unity,) if $m = (a_1, a_2, \ldots a_0)(1, i, i^2)(1, j, j^2)$, $n = (b_1, b_2, \ldots b_0)(1, i, i^2)(1, j, j^2)$,—to find the relations between the a's and b's necessary and sufficient that $m^3 = n^3 = 1$ and $n m = \lambda m n$.

Professor Michelson.

(a) *The establishment of a light wave as the ultimate unit of length.*

Almost every accurate measurement involves and usually depends upon a comparison between standards of length. In order that the results obtained by the refined methods and instruments now in use may be tested and compared all over the world, it is very essential that all such measurements should be ultimately referred to *a single inalterable standard.*

At present the object is only approximately obtained by making a metal bar with finely ruled lines at the ends the ultimate standard at the temperature of melting ice. The length between these lines at the standard temperature is defined by law as the *standard meter*, and the bar is carefully guarded in a vault where it is never handled except for comparison with *copies.*

Copies of the standard which constitute secondary standards are issued to the principal countries.

This system has been found sufficiently accurate for all but the most delicate work, and if the *permanence* of the standard could be relied upon, leaves but little room for improvement.

But it is well-known that all material bodies are undergoing changes of form, of volume, of weight — even of structure — changes which are altogether inappreciable except by very delicate measurements—but which, in the course of years, may accumulate until they are of sufficient magnitude to vitiate the results of years of patient labor.

Some time ago it was thought possible to remedy this defect by selecting some " natural " standard which should be as permanent as the earth itself.

Two such attempts were made and both were unsuccessful; —the first was the measurement of the length of a pendulum vibrating in one second at Paris; and, second, the measurement of the forty millionth part of the earth's circumference.

It was found that the results obtained in both cases differed among themselves by quantities much greater than are now admissible. Even if this difficulty were remedied by greater care and more perfect instruments, it may still be objected that both results would depend on the form and size of the earth and its time of rotation, all of which are subject to change.

A third method has been proposed which depends on the fundamental properties of the atoms and the universal ether. Scientific men agree that there is no change in these, within the limits of the visible universe.

This method proposes the *length of a light wave* produced by the vibrations of the atoms of any convenient kind of matter in the state of incandescent vapor, and transmitted to the eye by the luminiferous ether.

The very fact which permits an extraordinary degree of accuracy in this method, namely, the minuteness of the light waves, is at the same time the chief difficulty in making it a practical standard. Thus to *multiply* so small a length as a fifty thousandth of an inch to the length of a yard or a meter without at the same time multiplying the errors, is the problem which has hitherto yielded only partially to the patience and ingenuity of physicists.

In view of some very satisfactory results obtained by the "wave-comparer" in some preliminary work, it is hoped that these difficulties have been so far overcome that when the present investigation is completed, a method will be devised which will enable two observers at opposite ends of the earth, with different instruments and entirely independently, to construct two standards containing say a million light waves, which shall not differ from each other so much as do the present copies from the original standard.

It may be stated that the new method has already attracted the attention of physicists generally, and in particular of the International Bureau of Weights and measures, and it is hoped that the demonstration of its practicability will be soon followed by its universal adoption.

(b) *The application of interference methods to astronomical measurements.*

It is well known that the "resolving power" of a telescope increases in proportion to the diameter of its object-glass. Thus in the case of a close double-star, if the angle subtended by the components is one second of arc, it would require a four inch glass to recognize it as a double. The largest telescope in the world would scarcely suffice to separate the components, if the angle were less than a tenth of a second.

The same statements apply also to the case of a minute disc, such as is subtended by a small planet or satellite; so that if this subtended an angle less than a tenth of a second, it would be impossible to say from its appearance whether it was a planetoid or a star.

The stars themselves are so far distant that, notwithstanding their great size, they look like mere points, even in the largest telescopes, and, as it is tolerably safe to say, that since there are practical difficulties in the way of increasing the size of the glasses which increase enormously faster than the dimensions, it is simply hopeless to arrive at any idea of the real size of these distant luminaries by this means alone.

As a result of a preliminary investigation completed last year in the Physical Laboratory of Clark University, it has been shown that by the simple device of covering the telescope by a cap provided with two adjustable slits, the capabilities of the instrument for such measurements may be increased from fifty to one hundred times. As instances of the performance of this arrangement, the following observations may be cited. Two minute holes in a piece of platinum foil, only one two hundred and fiftieth of an inch apart, were viewed at a distance of a hundred feet through an excellent four-inch telescope (for the use of which thanks are due to the kindness of Dr. Kimball of the Worcester Polytechnic Institute.) By this means, it could barely be distinguished that the holes were double — no measurement was possible. On making the measurement by means of the device mentioned, the distance between the holes was correctly ascertained to within two or three per cent. Again, on viewing a single opening, only one fiftieth of an inch in diameter the apparent diameter was found to be in error by from fifty to one hundred per cent.; whereas, the new method gave results correct to within two per cent.

Finally the arrangement has been further modified so as to dispense entirely with the large telescope, thus making it possible to increase the size of the instrument almost without limit. If among the nearer fixed stars there is any as large as our sun, it would subtend an angle of about one hundredth of a second of arc; and the corresponding diameter of telescope required to observe this small angle is forty feet, which, while utterly out of question as regards a telescope objective, is still perfectly feasible with the device in question. There is, however, no inherent improbability of stars presenting a much larger angle than this; and the possibility of gaining some positive knowledge of the real size of these distant luminaries would more than repay the time, care and patience which it would be necessary to bestow on such a work.

It may be added in conclusion that by the kindness of Professor Pickering, the director of Harvard College Observatory, the six inch equatorial and such conveniences as the observatory affords, are to be employed in testing the new plan at once upon the heavenly bodies.

MR. ALEXANDER MCADIE.

From the opening of the University until the arrival of the apparatus kindly loaned by the Chief Signal Officer General Greely, Mr. McAdie has spent his time in the preparation of a monograph on the Aurora, using the observations of the International Polar Expeditions of 1881-2-3, particularly the Lady Franklin Bay, the Point Barrow, and the Danish and Swedish expeditions. This is nearly ready for publication, but his preference is to hold it and incorporate it at a later date in a book on Atmospheric Electricity.

Plans and specifications for a multiple quadrant electrometer were drawn up and later designs and specifications for an improved electrometer battery. The electrometer was constructed by Brashear and is satisfactory.

There are a great many points in connection with the intensity and duration of the lightning flash,—that this instrument could throw light upon, and as far as the work went last year, it was eminently satisfactory. In March, with the arrival of the electrometers of the Geneva Society, (these electrometers are Mascart's modification of Sir Wm. Thomson's quadrant electrometer as further modified by the U. S. Signal Service; plans and specification for which Mr. McAdie drew up when in the laboratory of the Signal Office, under Prof. Mendenhall) the work of obtaining a continuous record of the electrical potential of the air began. These results have been worked up, and the paper is about ready for the press ; as it stands at present, it would make a pamphlet of about 40 pages.

Mr. McAdie has also published a prize essay on Tornadoes, and several minor communications in "Nature," and the "American Meteorological Journal," also has the "roughs" of five small papers. 1. On Color-Blindness. 2. Dust in the Atmosphere. 3. Weather Charts. 4. Cyclones and Tornadoes. 5. Thunder-Storms. A translation of Mascart's long paper in the "Journal de Physique, January, 1890," printed in "Am. Meteor. Journ., May, 1890."

III.—CHEMISTRY.

DR. J. U. NEF.

Dr. J. U. Nef, with the assistance of Dr. Victor Pæpcke, has been at work during the year 1889–90 on research in organic chemistry. The results obtained have been in great part published as follows :

1st. "On Tautomeric Compounds," American Chemical Journal, Vol. XII, 6, pp. 47. Ueber Tautomere Körper." Liebig's Annalen der Chemie, 258, pp. 261–318.

2nd. "The Constitution of Benzoquinone," American Chemical Journal, Vol. XII, 7, pp. 26.

It is impossible to explain to any one not familiar with organic chemistry the importance or the bearing of the above lines of work.

The long series of experiments with tautomeric compounds, which have been chiefly in the Succinylosuccinic acid group, have come to a definite conclusion. There are in this group a large number of substances which have the property of existing in two, three or more different geometrical forms. This peculiarity has lead some chemists to believe that the different forms correspond to different chemical molecules. It was possible here, as in many other cases, to make the assumption of tautomerism, i. e., of a mobile hydrogen atom which can wander from carbon to oxygen or vice versa ad libitum. The experimental results have proved conclusively that the hypothesis is false in the above case and besides have brought forward new views and facts, concerning tautomeric compounds in general—

The absence of tautomerism in the Anilic acid series has been definitely proven ; it also has become exceedingly probable that acetoacetic ether, which has so long been regarded by the majority of chemists as a Ketone, is really an alcohol and not tautomeric at all. The Phenyl-hydrazine reaction, which has heretofore been regarded as a rigid proof of the existence of a Ketone or an aldehyde group, is no longer conclusive.

The assumption of the wandering of the hydrogen atom in a molecule so generally made to suit the reagent or hypothesis applied is thus rendered very improbable.

The work on the constitution of benzoquinone has had for its object the determination of the exact chemical structure of the molecule of this substance. Since its discovery by Wosrekensky in 1839, a very large number of facts have accumulated concerning quinone and its many derivatives. Quinone is interesting because of its peculiar properties, being a strong oxidizing agent and having a pungent smell like dilute chlorine. Up to the present time three formulae have been put forward as representing its constitution:

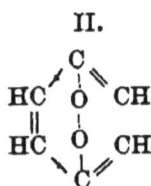

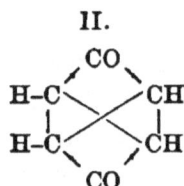

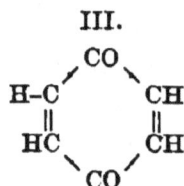

II. II. III.

Hyperoxide formula. Diagonal Ketone formula of Claus. Ketone formula of Fittig.

By a series of experiments with the anilic acids it was found that the results were decidedly in favor of Fittig's formula (III) and finally it was found that quinone itself adds one and two molecules of bromine, forming peculiar addition products, which proves conclusively that it is an unsaturated body like ethylene, and that therefore it contains two doubly bound carbon atoms. Since quinone is a very simple substance, as well known as benzene, the question of its constitution is of general interest.

One of the most striking results obtained in the work on quinone, was that certain hexamethylene derivatives (or closed chains of six constituent carbon atoms) are decomposed instantly by means of pure water with the same violence as a carbonate by mineral acids, and thereby are converted with evolution of carbonic acid into pentamethylene derivatives or closed claims of five constituent carbon atoms.

DR. LOEB.

The delays in making and placing his somewhat elaborate apparatus, prevented active work until late in the academic year. Some experiments were made on the oxidization and reduction of iron salts in the magnetic field, the results of which will soon be published. For more than a hundred years it has been a favorite speculation with English and American chemists, whether the phenomena of magnetism are so closely related to those of chemical affinity, that the one would influence the other. While various experiments have been made, at different times, whose results were now favorable and now unfavorable to such an assumption, it appeared that all of them were rather complicated by the introduction of processes, like the change from the solid to the liquid state, involving a new set of physical effects. To obviate such difficulties Dr. Loeb cast about for a reaction involving no *physical* changes ; such a one would be the oxidation of a ferrous to a ferric salt in solution, as the ferric salts are more magnetic than the corresponding ferrous. If magnetism really affects chemical reactions, it might be assumed to hasten such a reaction; while it ought to retard a reaction which tended to lower the magnetism of the solution by the reduction of the iron. Numerous series of careful observations, under varied conditions, convinced him that no noticeable difference is produced in these reactions by the presence of a powerful magnetic field, and he is inclined to consider this a proof of some moment in support of those who deny the existence of close relations between magnetism and chemical action. This question will be approached from a a different standpoint the coming year.

DR. MUTHMANN.

Dr. Muthmann was occupied with researches on isomorphous mixtures of different organic and inorganic bodies. A publication, concerning *Sodic naphtylamine—and naphtylhydrazine sulphonate*, which was finished together with Dr. W. Ramsay in Munich is printed in the September issue of "Groth's Zeitschrift für Krystallographie." It contains observations on the subject, obtained by Lehmann's microscope, and will increase our knowledge of isomorphous mixtures as well as of polymorphism.

Dr. Muthmann's main task last year, to investigate the

crystallographical relations between *potassium perchlorate and permanganate.* Researches on this object were begun by Prof. Groth 25 years ago; his observations are contained in a publication in "Poggendorf's Annalen." Dr. Muthmann's investigations have shown that all the former measurements of the crystals in question are not exact enough to give a sufficient material for solving the important question, how mixed crystals are built up, his results being a new idea of the subject, of which the following is a description:

Formerly crystallographers believed that the angles of mixed crystals differ from those of the pure substances; Italian mineralogists, (and also Rammelsberg) assert that the angle of a mixture is between the corresponding angles of the pure substances, while Groth says, in his publication, that it is often larger or smaller than that shown by either component. Dr. Muthmann's measurements gave the unexpected result that both opinions are false and that for instance a good crystal, containing potassic perchlorate and permanganate, has exactly the same angles as one of the pure substances; with which of them it is conform depends on the quantity of each salt in the mixture. This result was so unexpected that Prof. Groth, at present the greatest authority in crystallographical questions, with whom he had a long interview and correspondence on the matter, thinks it desirable to ascertain the above given result by observations on other salts. He will augment the observations on ferrous and copper sulphate. He hopes to be ready with these measurements very soon.

A research on rare earths is in preparation, which will be begun after he has finished his work on mixed crystals.

DR. WILLIAMS.

Dr. Williams has been engaged during the greater part of the year in the investigation of the rocks and minerals of the State of Arkansas and especially of those of the Magnet Cove region.

The time from October 9 to January 1 was occupied with the field work, which was done in co-öperation with the State Geological Survey. The three principal areas, where igneous rocks occur, were carefully gone over, and the limits of the various rocks noted on the fine topographical prepared by the state survey especially for this purpose.

On returning to Worcester, Dr. Williams immediately began the investigation and determination of the rocks and minerals brought back with him, some of which proved to be of great interest.

The investigation of the rock has been carried on by means of numerous chemical analysis, both of the rock as a whole, and of the separate minerals found in it; and by means of a large suite of thin sections — numbering nearly 500 in all — which have allowed of a very complete insight into the micro-scopical structure of the various kinds of rocks found in the state.

Among the minerals which have been the subjects of separate investigations may be mentioned the following:

Eudialyte. Discovered at Magnet Cove by Shepard, in 1861, but lost sight of until a year ago, when Hidden and Mackin-tosh published a note describing some grains of a red mineral from this locality, and suggesting their identity with the Eudialyte of Shepard. The first measurements of crystals from this locality were made in the mineralogical laboratory of the University, and showed the complete identity of the mineral with the already well-known Eudialyte.

Eucolite. This is found associated with Eudialyte, and is its first appearance in America. It has been found that a single crystal may consist in part of Eucolite while the rest of it is made up of Eudialyte.

These results are awaiting publication in the *American Journal of Science.*

Leucite. The occurrence of this mineral in Arkansas was first suggested by G. F. Kunz, on the strength of an analysis by F. A. Genth. At that time the mineral had only been found in isolated crystals and has only lately been found in the rock. It has been shown by analyzing first that portion of the mineral which is soluble in hydrochloric acid and then the insoluble part, that, although possessing the crystal form of Leucite, the mineral is, in reality, made up of a mixture of Sanidine and Nepheline. A complete analysis of the material taken from a very pure white crystal, differs somewhat from

Genth's analysis, because the latter was made from very impure material, so impure, in fact, that Kunz thought it not improbable that the mineral was the result of the alteration of the common garnet of the region.

These results and a description of the rock in which the Leucite occurs will be published in the *American Journal of Science.*

Vesuvianite. The chemical, crystallographical and optical examination of beautiful crystals of this mineral found in a metamorphosed limestome have proven its identity, and have shown it to be remarkable on account of the large number of small quartz crystals included in it.

Mangano pectolite. This is a new mineral which is very similar to Pectolite, but differs from the latter; in that it contains over 4.3% of Manganese. Its properties have been more fully studied than those of Pectolite itself, on account of the greater ease with which comparatively large single crystals may be obtained.

A full account of this crystal will be published in *Groth's Zeitschrift für Mineralogie und Krystallographie.*

Many commoner minerals have been determined and described, which have not as yet been known from Magnet Cove or else have been mistaken for other species. Among these may be mentioned Fluorite (chlorophane), Apatite, Titanite, and several forms of Mica.

The principal part of the work has, however, been the study of the rock sections under the microscope, and as yet there can nothing positive be said about them. They cover a large range of rock species, but as the study of them is, by no means, completed, no conclusions regarding their relations to each other or even of their mineralogical composition can be drawn. These results will form a volume of the report of the State Geological Survey of Arkansas.

No inconsiderable part of the time has been occupied in the preparation of maps and in reviewing the literature on the subject of the rocks and minerals of Arkansas.

Outside of his Arkansas work, Dr. Williams has been busy in examining and describing some peculiar specimens of quartz from various localities sent to him by G. F. Kunz of

New York, and he hopes to soon be able to publish a paper on the results of his investigations.

MR. JULIUS STIEGLITZ.

Dr. Stieglitz, under the direction of Dr. Nef, began a series of experiments with the idea of obtaining new carboxylated derivatives of quinone. Such derivatives were first obtained by Dr. Nef, who showed that they were very unstable. The method employed consisted in treating chloranil and dibromo quinone terephtalic ether, with sodium malonic ether. Thereby ethers of new acids of the desired nature were obtained. All attempts to prepare the free acids from the new ethers proved futile and yielded simple products of decomposition. The results obtained so far contribute to confirm the supposition that benzoquinone carbonic acids can not be obtained as stable compounds. The work is not complete, but a preliminary report is to be published in the American Chemical Journal in Baltimore, under the title "On Benzoquinone Carbonic Acids."

IV.—DEPARTMENT OF BIOLOGY.

A.—ANIMAL MORPHOLOGY.

PROFESSOR WHITMAN.

Historical Research.—My work in research has been partly historical, partly embryological. The larger portion of the academic year was devoted to the two following subjects : (1). *Theories of Generation,* from the times of Aristotle to the present. (2.) *The Development of Comparative Anatomy,* beginning with Severino and ending with the celebrated discussions of 1830, between Cruvier and Geoffroy St. Hilaire. This portion of my work is still very far from completion ; and several years more will be required before the hoped for results can be reached.

We have a considerable number of works devoted to these subjects ; but most of them are purely descriptive and quite inadequate to the needs of the present time.

My aim has been, not to accumulate disconnected facts and details in chronological sequence, but to trace the continuity of development in biological philosophy and discovery—to find the origin of the ideas, doctrines, systems, and schools that have marked the more important epochs, and to bring them into organic connection with the biological knowledge of to-day.

It may be well to state here some of the considerations which have led me to undertake such work. My own need as teacher and investigator has been the prime inducement. I have searched in vain among extant treatises of the subjects above named for the information desired. The same need and the same difficulties have been quite generally experienced, as I am assured from many sources. It has seemed to me, therefore, that work in the direction indicated might lead to results that would be generally useful to biological students, investigators, and teachers.

I find another strong inducement in the fact that our work here is to be limited exclusively to investigation. The instruction required to make the most successful investigators and teachers must certainly include the history of the science. Every science represents a long continued advance; and to be understood, it must be viewed as an organic growth. Its present stage is comprehensible only after we have studied carefully the antecedent stages of germination and development. Early discoveries and ideas are not simply superseded, they are rather incorporated, absorbed, and extended in the later ones.

The fullest appreciation of the extent and value of our "vast patrimony of science" implies, therefore, a thorough knowledge of the steps of its acquisition. The historical survey brings before us not only past progress, but also present form and state, aims and prospects. It illuminates the field, gives breadth and depth to our conceptions, enriches and enlarges our general views, makes us more generous, considerate, and respectful towards our predecessors and contemporaries. It furnishes stimulating examples, suggests new ideas and methods, enables us to avoid the errors of the past, places before us the problems that have been solved and those that still await solution, and so saves us from wasting energy in reproducing facts already established.

Embryological Research.—My embryological work has consisted in tracing the early development of the egg of one of our large Salamanders (*Necturus maculatus*). Necturus, as the genus was called by Rafinesque, has its nearest living ally in the subterranean Proteus of Europe. It is the lowest representative of American Batrachia, and thus holds an important place in the ancestral history of the vertebrates. It has characters intermediate between the fishes on the one hand and the lowest air-breathing vertebrates on the other; and stands in the direct line of descent connecting extinct forms of the Carboniferous period and the higher Salamanders of to-day. Unusual interest, therefore, centers in the embryology of this animal. Material for such study has long been sought for by naturalists, but hitherto without success.

Necturus is found only in North America, but here it has a

wide range, being distributed through the tributaries of the Great Lakes and of the Mississippi, and in the rivers and lakes of many of the Southern States. I have found it quite abundant in the smaller lakes of Wisconsin, and it is there that my material has been collected.

The egg of Necturus is about the size of a pea; and unlike the eggs of most Batrachia, it has no pigment to obscure the processes of development. Its large size, absence of pigment, and the transparency of its envelopes render it a peculiarly favorable object for the study of the superficial aspects of development. On the other hand, the preparation of material for preservation presents much greater difficulties than are met with in any other amphibian egg that has thus far been investigated.

After many experiments, I finally succeeded in overcoming many of these difficulties and in preserving an abundance of material for the study of all stages from the moment of deposit up to the time when the embryo begins to form. Careful drawings of all these stages were made, and it only remains to complete the study by means of sections of preserved eggs.

One of the more important points which I hope to be able to settle by this study is that of the formation of the embryo. I am now able to show substantial agreement in this respect between the fishes and the amphibia. The mode of formation of the vertebrate embryo has been much studied and much discussed, but still many obscurities remain to be cleared up. Necturus promises to throw some light on this problem.

I have, further, devoted considerable attention to the habits of Necturus, and have the data for a pretty complete account. Hitherto, it has been considered impossible to distinguish the sexes by any external appearances. This point has now been satisfactorily settled, and it has opened the way for another investigation. Full details will be given when my memoir is published.

Marine Biological Laboratory.—During the summer, the following researches have been carried on under my direction, at the Marine Biological Laboratory, at Wood's Holl:

1. Contributions to the Morphology of the Vertebrate Head.

2. The Development of the Lateral-Line System of Sense-Organs in Batrachus.

3. The Sense-Organs of the Pectoral Appendages of one of the Gurnards.

4. The Early Stages of Development in Spirorbis.

5. The Origin of the Periblast in Fundulus.

6. The First Stages in the Development of Some Marine Mollusks.

7. The Origin and Significance of Kupffer's Vesicle.

In this work I have had the assistance of Dr. McMurrich and Dr. Ayers. The first of these memoirs is ready for publication; the others will be continued at the next session.

Editorial Work.—During the year two numbers of the *Journal of Morphology* have been issued, and two more are now in press. The department of Microscopy in the *American Naturalist* has continued under my charge. The purpose of this department is to report all important advances in methods of investigation. A volume of biological lectures, delivered by the staff and other members of the Marine Laboratory during the summer, is soon to be published.

DR. MCMURRICH.

During the past University Session Dr. McMurrich devoted his attention to certain problems concerning the relationship of certain groups of the lower many-celled animals. A large number of forms have been grouped together under the name of Actiniaria or Sea Anemones ; a more thorough study of the structure of the animals included within the group has shown, however, that it is necessary to sub-divide it into several co-ordinate groups, each distinctly marked out, so far as the adult animal is concerned, by characteristic anatomical peculiarities. A more accurate knowledge of these peculiarities is exceedingly important for the elucidation of the interrelationships of the various groups, and the early part of the session was employed in a study of the anatomical features of a large number of Actinians obtained by the U. S. Fish Commission Steamer "Albatross," on a voyage to San Francisco during the winter of 1887–8. Many important facts have been derived from this study, and it will be continued during the coming session. The collection contains a large number of undescribed species, many of which are of peculiar interest as representatives of the deep-sea fauna of the Pacific, having been dredged in depths varying from 400 to 1,500 fathoms.

The same problem was also attacked from the embryological side with very important results. The material for this research was obtained partly at the Marine Laboratories of the Johns Hopkins University at Beaufort, N. C., and at Nassau, Bahama Islands, W. I., and partly at the Marine Biological Laboratory at Wood's Holl, Mass., and consisted of early developmental stages of forms belonging to four different groups of Actinians. A study of it demonstrated that, notwithstanding the great dissimilarity of the adult forms of the various groups, at one period of their development they were very similar, and thus it has been possible to trace out the ancestry and evolution of the various groups. The results of this investigation are now nearly ready for publication, and will probably appear during the coming winter.

In connection with this work, some general considerations were suggested regarding the primitive differentiation of the tissues of the many-celled animals. These ideas were discussed in a lecture delivered at the Marine Biological Laboratory during the past summer and will shortly appear in print.

A thorough study was also made of a peculiar Actinian *Cerianthus.* Hitherto no American forms of this genus had been studied, and the investigation of *C. Americanus,* brought to light many interesting points of difference from its European relatives, and, at the same time, threw considerable light on the affinities and characteristics of the group to which it belongs. An account of this investigation is now in print.

During the past summer Dr. McMurrich was enabled (thanks to the facilities afforded by the Marine Biological Laboratory at Wood's Holl, Mass.,) to extend his studies to another group of forms somewhat related to the Actinians, namely, the Jelly fishes. Material illustrative of the development of the large *Cyanea arctica* was obtained in considerable abundance and preserved for study. Part of this was worked over at Wood's Holl during the summer, and it is hoped that the investigation may be concluded during the coming winter.

Material was also collected and preserved for the investigation of the embryology of the Isopods, a group of Crustacea, of whose development and affinities comparatively little is known, and also of the Ixodidæ or Ticks, whose embryology is likewise very little known.

DR. BUMPUS.

The year was mainly spent in studying the breeding habits and the embryological development of the American lobster.

Numbers of living lobsters were kept in confinement during the autumn and winter, both at Nahant and at Wood's Holl, Mass., and points of both scientific and economic interest were established.

During the spring and summer, through the courtesy of the U. S. Fish Commission, several hundred egg-bearing lobsters were examined, and experiments on artificially hatching the spawn were carried on. The most important embryological results, however, were obtained through the Marine Biological Laboratory. Every possible facility was there provided for the successful prosecution of embryological work. A full account of this work, its methods and results, will soon appear in the *American Journal of Morphology.*

B.—ANATOMY.

The greater portion of the last academic year was devoted to the study of connective tissue fibrils. Until recently but two kinds of fibrils were known to form the frame-work of the body of vertebrates. The white fibrous, the strongest organic tissue known, (e. g. tendon) and the yellow elastic interwoven in the portions of the body which are elastic (e. g. arteries). To these two sets of fibrils Dr. Mall has added a third ; a tissue widely distributed and found in nearly all organs,—the mucous membranes, liver and kidney. In these it constitutes the whole frame-work. He has succeeded in isolating the fibrils in large quantity, and finds marked chemical difference between them and the white fibrous and elastic fibers. Towards the close of the year methods were found by which these fibrils can be stained, thus permitting very careful microscopic examination. In a short time these observations will be shown before the Royal Society of Saxony, and will be published in Leipsic and in Baltimore.

These fibrils and their properties were discovered while the histology of the portal system was being investigated. These studies have yielded valuable results regarding the minute anatomy and history of the liver lobule. The aim has constantly been to study the relation of the microscopic parts to one another, and the architecture of these individual parts.

In a study of this kind the blood-vessels are constantly met with, and these have proven to be of most valuable service in his investigation. He has traced and counted the many million of channels a drop of blood may take while passing through the organs of digestion. It is natural while studying a system of tubes like this to inquire into the forces which undoubtedly influence the circulation during digestion and rest. It is impossible to conceive that such a set of tubes with lining walls should be absolutely passive. Several years ago he found that intestinal contraction played a very important part in the circulation through its walls. During the last summer while continuing his investigation in the laboratory of Prof. Ludwig, a nerve was discovered which acts as a vaso-constrictor of the portal vein. Not only does this strike the key-note of his investigation, but it also throws new light on, and opens up a new field in the physiology of circulation. A preliminary report of this operation will soon appear in the *Arch. f. Phys.*, Berlin.

The laboratory has also been fitted up with the necessary material for modelling microscopic objects after the method of Born. Some three months were occupied in modelling a human embryo less than a month old. The extreme difficulty to obtain perfect specimens of this age justifies him in devoting so much time to a single, apparently insignificant, specimen. The individual studies of this kind have placed humam embryology equally as high as that of any of the lower animals.

Dr. Gage has been conducting a series of experiments upon intestinal suture. It is known by experiment that operations are more successful upon lower animals than upon man. Starting with the methods known to surgeons, he applied them in his experiments and then attempted to improve. Improvements in turn can be applied in human surgery. The experiments of recent years have thrown much light upon intestinal surgery and make of it a science. His experiments have been varied and he finds that by certain methods all animals may be saved provided they are operated upon within a short time after an injury.

Dr. Miller has been studying the histology of the lung and the relation of the blood-vessels to the air-cells. His work has already demonstrated the relation of the air-cells to one another.

Dr. Tuckerman has spent the entire year in studying the gustatory organ of mammalia, the results of which will appear in the next number of the *American Journal of Morphology*, Twenty nine species of animals were studied, and the structures of their gustatory organs described and compared. The paper concludes with a comparison of the gustatory papillæ and taste bulbs of the marsupalia and endentata.

C.—PHYSIOLOGY.

DR. LOMBARD.

Most of the year has been spent in investigations on fatigue. Valuable results have been found, but are not yet ready for publication.

DR. CARDWELL.

Dr. Cardwell spent the year in experimental researches on the study of the functions of the cerebellum, and reports satisfactory progress.

V.—DEPARTMENT OF PSYCHOLOGY.

A—NEUROLOGY.

DR. DONALDSON

has been engaged during the year in describing the brain of the deaf-mute, Laura Bridgman, and the first part of his results will occupy about 50 pages in the forthcoming number of the *American Journal of Psychology*. The summer has been largely spent in studying variations in the weight and volume of the human brain according to the method by which it is preserved, but these results are not yet ready for publication.

DR. HODGE.

The special work of last year was directed to the investigation of the process of recovery from effects of fatigue in the cells of the spinal ganglia. Up to last year the changes which occur in nerve cells during fatigue had been pretty well made out. The next step, of even greater importance than the first, must be a knowledge of the processes concerned in recovery. It was not known, although we had strong reasons for supposing, that nerve cells recover at all after fatigue.

A series of five animals has been obtained; in each of which certain nerve cells have been worked under exactly similar conditions for five hours, and afterwards, allowed to rest respectively, 0 hours, 6 hours, 12 hours, 18 hours and 24 hours, with a view to determining the process of recovery and also the length of time requisite for recovery from the effects of five hours work.

Examination of the tissue is still in progress, but sufficient evidence has been obtained to demonstrate that—

1. Individual nerve cells do recover from the effect of fatigue.

2. The process of recovery is a slow one.

As far as the determination has been carried, we may say that after six hours of complete rest, the nerve cells have about half recovered from the effects of five hours rather severe work. At the end of 24 hours they have wholly recovered. The publication of this chapter of the subject it is hoped may be made in full early this fall.

B.—EXPERIMENTAL PSYCHOLOGY.

DR. SANFORD

has devised and described in the *Journal of Psychology* a simple and inexpensive chronoscope,—measuring with tolerable exactness to one one-hundredth of a second. He has also some studies on the relation of the reaction-time to the way in which the response is made, which are well advanced and which he proposes to publish during the coming year, in connection with further work in the same line. Dr. Sanford has also assisted in editorial work upon the *Journal of Psychology*, conducted and edited by the president of the University.

MR. HERBERT NICHOLS

has concluded an important research on the effect of habit upon time-judgments. After performing the experiments which show the existence of such an effect, he undertook a second series designed to show whether the practice (ultimately resulting in the habit) left its impress chiefly centrally or peripherally, and whether on the sensory or motor mechanism. Mr. Nichols is at present engaged upon a resumè of the history of the Psychology of Time. This study, together with the experimental and critical portions of his work, will soon be ready for publication.

Mr. E. A. Kirkpatrick has published, under President Hall's direction, and from data collected by him, a study on College Seniors and Electives in Psychological Subjects, *American Journal of Psychology*, Vol. III, No. 2.

C.—ANTHROPOLOGY.

DR. BOAS

has been engaged since a number of years in researches on the Indians of the North Pacific coast, the work having for its object a thorough investigation of the physical character, religious belief, customs and languages of the numerous tribes of that region. The material for these researches has been collected in four journeys to the North Pacific coast. His researches during the past year have been mainly on those lines and on the material collected on his journeys. In the beginning of the academic year a large collection of myths and traditions from Alaska and British Columbia was arranged and prepared for publication; it will probably be published in the near future. In discussing these myths an attempt has been made to trace their history and growth and evidence is brought forward tending to show that certain legends have been carried from tribe to tribe all over the American continent, while others tend to show that diffusion of legends also took place between Northeastern Asia and Northwest America. After the completion of this manuscript more special lines of research were taken up. The material collected in the summer of 1889 was sifted and arranged and the results briefly described in a report to the British Association for the Advancement of Science which was presented at its meeting at Leeds in September, 1890. The report treats on the distribution, social organization, customs, beliefs and languages of the tribes of the northern part of Vancouver Island and of the southern part of the interior of British Columbia. Work on an osteological collection from the North Pacific coast was also begun. The last month of the academic year was spent in preparatory studies for a journey to Oregon, Washington and British Columbia.

MR. C. A. ORR.

Mr. Orr was sent as Anthropologist on the Government Eclipse Expedition to Loanda and was well equipped with apparatus and material. He has not yet returned, but, leaving the expedition, has penetrated into the heart of Africa northward from Cape Town.

D.—HISTORICAL PSYCHOLOGY.

MR. B. C. BURT

spent some time in preparing a needed text book on the History of Modern Philosophy. He endeavored to set forth the platonic doctrine of the unity of opposites as a rational explanation of the unity of the world, and printed two articles on the General History of Philosophy since Hegel, laying great stress upon the importance of Hartmann's work.

DR. ALFRED COOK

investigated the fundamental principles of the Kantean philosophy which he finds to be identity, change and motion, and hence he argues fundamental agreement between Kant and the laws of motion, as defined by Maxwell. Dr. Cook also began, and has nearly finished, a text book in general psychology, which he believes to be needed and which attempts to harmonize the conflicting tendencies in this field.

MR. DICKINSON MILLER

spent a good part of the year in the historical investigation of how far Kant had solved the difficulties broached by Hume. He reached the conclusion that Kant had failed in his effort to give a rational basis for primary beliefs, and that these first principles all rest solely upon the non-rational basis of instinct. His work will eventually be published as a study of Kant's theory of knowledge.

E.—CRIMINOLOGY.

DR. MACDONALD

has prepared and printed digests of many of the leading contributions to criminology during the last ten years, thus bringing this material together and within reach of criminologists and psychologists generally; so scattered is this literature in books and periodicals, in many languages, that this work has long been a desideratum. In his visits to institutions, Dr. MacDonald has collected some material for the study of pure, or type—cases among the various classes of criminals and defectives.

F.—EDUCATION.

DR. BURNHAM

was sent by the University to study European institutions and to collect literature for the new educational department. He visited many institutions in Great Britain, France, Germany and Belgium, and collected many reports and other literary material.

www.ingramcontent.com/pod-product-compliance
Lightning Source LLC
Chambersburg PA
CBHW022039080426
42733CB00007B/900